DATE DUE		
MAY 15 2003	NOV 0 3 2005	
OCT 23 2003		
Nov 09 2003	FEB 01 2012	
AUG 12 2005		
FEB 22 2007		
APR 19 2011		

The Conflict Resolution Library

Dealing with Anger

• Marianne Johnston •

The Rosen Publishing Group's
PowerKids Press
New York

Published in 1996 by The Rosen Publishing Group, Inc.
29 East 21st Street, New York, NY 10010

Photo Credits: Cover by Maria Moreno; p. 11 by Thomas Mangieri; p.16 © Noble Stock/International Stock; all other photos by Maria Moreno.

First Edition

Johnston, Marianne.
    Dealing with anger / Marianne Johnston. — 1st ed.
        p.   cm. — (The conflict resolution library)
    Includes index.
    Summary: A discussion of anger including suggestions for ways to deal with it directly, channel it to something productive, and avoid its destructiveness.
    ISBN 0-8239-2325-8
    1. Anger—Juvenile literature. [1. Anger.] I. Title. II. Series.
BF575.A5J64   1996
152.4—dc20   95-50795
                                                 CIP
                                                 AC

Manufactured in the United States of America

Contents

What Is Anger?

Anger is a strong feeling. It can be scary and confusing. You can feel anger when someone does something you don't like, or when things don't go your way.

Everybody gets angry sometimes. Being angry doesn't mean you're a bad person. Anger is a natural feeling.

But anger can get you into trouble when you don't deal with it the right way.

◀ Everyone feels angry sometimes.

You're a Big Kid Now

When you were a baby, crying was the only way you could tell others you were angry. But it didn't tell others *why* you were angry.

Now that you're older, you can tell people why you are angry. This is a healthy way of letting out anger. When others understand what is making you upset, they can help you fix the problem. That way you will begin to feel better.

It's good to tell someone when ▶ you're angry with them.

Destructive Anger

It is good to let anger out. Sometimes people let it out the wrong way. Some people want to hit the person they are mad at. Anger is **destructive** (de-STRUK-tiv) when we hurt our things, ourselves, or other people.

If you feel like hitting when you get angry, stop and ask yourself, "Is hitting going to solve the problem?" The answer is always no. Hitting only makes everybody feel worse.

◀ Think before you take your anger out on something or someone.

Let's Talk It Out

Sometimes we have arguments. When you are arguing, you believe you are right. That's exactly what the other person thinks too. Both sides have to **compromise** (KOM-pro-mize).

When two people compromise, they both give in a little. They talk out the problem. Each person listens carefully to the other. That way, both sides get some of what they want, and no one is left feeling angry.

The first step in compromising is to listen to each other. ▶

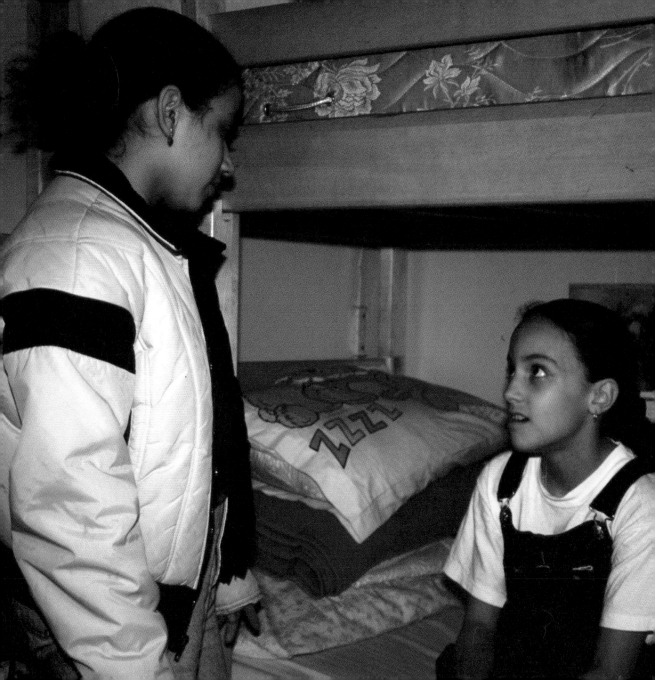

Emily and Alison

Alison was playing by herself. Her sister, Emily, wanted to play too. Alison wanted to be alone. She told Emily to go away, which made Emily angry. Alison got mad too.

Then Alison had a great idea! Alison told Emily that they could play together later if Emily would let Alison play by herself for an hour. Emily thought about it and agreed. They compromised. Both girls got part of what they wanted, and neither stayed angry.

◀ Compromising means that both people give in a little bit.

13

Positive Thinking

A good way to deal with anger is positive thinking. This means looking at the good side of things instead of the bad side.

When you have a good **outlook** (OWT-look) on life, you don't get angry very often. And when you do get angry, you use positive thinking to help you control your anger and think your way out of it.

One way to deal with anger is to look at the good side of things instead of the bad side. ▶

Richard and Terry

Richard and Terry were playing tag. Terry accidentally knocked Richard down. Richard's first reaction was anger. He wanted to knock Terry down too.

Then Richard thought about it. Terry was his best friend. He wouldn't knock Richard down on purpose. It must have been an accident.

Richard used positive thinking to deal with his anger, and so can you.

◄ Positive thinking helps you control your anger.

Frustration

Sometimes we get angry or **frustrated** (FRUS-tray-ted) when things don't happen the way we want them to. This kind of anger is different from being mad at someone.

When you are frustrated, find a place where you can be alone to think about the problem. Figure out what you are mad at. Then focus on the good side of the situation. You will calm down, and the frustration will begin to go away.

When you are frustrated, take some time to think about the problem. ▶

Baseball Blues

Rodney's baseball game didn't go well. All he could think about were his two strikeouts.

Rodney realized that he was angry because he had struck out. So instead he began to think about that great catch he made in the fourth inning. In fact, he had played well in the outfield the entire game.

After a while, Rodney noticed that his anger was gone and he felt better.

◀ Focusing on the bad parts of life can keep you from enjoying the good parts.

Using Your Anger

Sometimes anger can give you the strength to change a situation that you believe is wrong. You can use your anger to fix the problem.

Every day, Juan watched Henry, the school bully, pick on people. This made Juan angry. He decided to ask Henry to stop. Henry didn't listen. Juan told the principal about the situation. The next day, Henry left everyone alone.

Juan used his anger to help solve a problem.

Glossary

compromise (KOM-pro-mize) When two people work out an argument by giving in a little.

destructive (de-STRUK-tiv) Causing harm to yourself or others.

frustrated (FRUS-tray-ted) When you feel anger because things aren't happening the way you want them to.

outlook (OWT-look) How you look at situations in life.

Index